DINOSAUR FACT DIG

VELOCIRAPTOR
AND OTHER RAPTORS
THE NEED-TO-KNOW FACTS

BY

REBECCA RISSMAN

Consultant: Mathew J. Wedel, PhD
Associate Professor
Western University of Health Services

CAPSTONE PRESS
a capstone imprint

A+ Books are published by Capstone Press,
1710 Roe Crest Drive, North Mankato, Minnesota 56003
www.mycapstone.com

Library of Congress Cataloging-in-Publication Data
Rissman, Rebecca, author.
Velociraptor and other raptors / by Rebecca Rissman.
pages cm. – (A+ books. Dinosaur fact dig)
Audience: Ages 4–8.
Audience: K to grade 3.
Summary: "Full-color images and simple text introduce young readers to different raptor
dinosaurs, including their physical characteristics, habitats, and diets"– Provided by publisher.
Includes bibliographical references and index.
ISBN 978-1-4914-9651-0 (library binding)
ISBN 978-1-4914-9658-9 (paperback)
ISBN 978-1-4914-9664-0 (eBook PDF)
1. Velociraptor—Juvenile literature. 2. Dinosaurs—Juvenile literature. I. Title.
QE862.S3R5537 2016
567.91—dc23   2015028668

EDITORIAL CREDITS:
Michelle Hasselius, editor; Kazuko Collins, designer; Wanda Winch, media researcher;
Gene Bentdahl, production specialist

IMAGE CREDITS: All images by Jon Hughes except: MapArt (maps), Shutterstock: Elena
Elisseeva, green gingko leaf, Jiang Hongyan, yellow gingko leaf, Taigi, paper background

Printed in US.
007535CGS16

**NOTE TO PARENTS, TEACHERS,
AND LIBRARIANS:**
This Dinosaur Fact Dig book uses full-color
images and a nonfiction format to introduce
the concept of raptors. *Velociraptor and
Other Raptors* is designed to be read aloud
to a pre-reader or to be read independently
by an early reader. Images help listeners
and early readers understand the text and
concepts discussed. The book encourages
further learning by including the following
sections: Table of Contents, Glossary, Read
More, Internet Sites, Critical Thinking Using
the Common Core, and Index. Early readers
may need assistance using these features.

TABLE OF CONTENTS

Raptors were a fast, smart, and deadly group of dinosaurs. They slashed at prey with fierce teeth and razor sharp claws.

Raptors lived between 125 and 65 million years ago. Thanks to the film *Jurassic Park*, Velociraptor is one of the most well known raptors. But there were many other fierce raptors that roamed the earth. Learn about Microraptor, Buitreraptor, Bambiraptor, and other dinosaurs in the raptor group.

AVIMIMUS

PRONOUNCED: AH-vee-MY-mus

NAME MEANING: bird mimic

TIME PERIOD LIVED: Late Cretaceous Period, about 80 to 70 million years ago

LENGTH: 3.5 feet (1.1 meters)

WEIGHT: 25 pounds (11 kilograms)

TYPE OF EATER: omnivore

PHYSICAL FEATURES: feathers, long legs, short arms, and a beak

AVIMIMUS had claws on its hands and feet. It used them when hunting small animals. The dinosaur also ate plants.

Avimimus lived in the deserts of China and Mongolia.

N
W — E
S

where this dinosaur lived

AVIMIMUS looked like a bird. It was covered with feathers but couldn't fly.

AVIMIMUS could run very quickly. Its short, strong tail helped it balance while running.

BAMBIRAPTOR

PRONOUNCED: BAM-bee-RAP-tur

NAME MEANING: named after the character in the Disney movie *Bambi* because of its small size

TIME PERIOD LIVED: Late Cretaceous Period, about 75 million years ago

LENGTH: 30 inches (0.8 m)

WEIGHT: 4.5 pounds (2 kg)

TYPE OF EATER: carnivore

PHYSICAL FEATURES: traveled on two legs, had feathers

BAMBIRAPTOR could move its arms the way birds move their wings. But it could not fly.

BAMBIRAPTOR was a small, smart predator.

Some scientists believe **BAMBIRAPTOR** fossils are actually from a baby Saurornitholestes.

BAMBIRAPTOR fossils were first discovered in 1995.

BAMBIRAPTOR may have been able to climb trees.

Bambiraptor lived in what is now Montana.

N
W E
S

■ where this dinosaur lived

BEIPIAOSAURUS

PRONOUNCED: bay-pyow-SAWR-us

NAME MEANING: Beipiao lizard, because fossils were discovered near Beipiao, China

TIME PERIOD LIVED: Early Cretaceous Period, about 127 to 121 million years ago

LENGTH: 6 feet (1.8 m)

WEIGHT: 90 pounds (41 kg)

TYPE OF EATER: herbivore

PHYSICAL FEATURES: feathers, short legs, strong arms, and a beak

BEIPIAOSAURUS used its long claws to pull down leaves from trees and protect itself from predators.

BEIPIAOSAURUS used its strong beak to eat leaves and fruit.

BEIPIAOSAURUS was covered in long, brightly colored feathers. The dinosaur may have used its feathers to communicate with other dinosaurs.

Beipiaosaurus lived in the forests of what is now China.

■ where this dinosaur lived

BUITRERAPTOR

PRONOUNCED: BWEE-tree-RAP-tur

NAME MEANING: vulture thief

TIME PERIOD LIVED: Cretaceous Period, about 90 million years ago

LENGTH: 2 to 5 feet (0.6 to 1.5 m)

WEIGHT: 6.6 pounds (3 kg)

TYPE OF EATER: carnivore

PHYSICAL FEATURES: small body, feathers, and two short wings

It took scientists 10 days to dig the first **BUITRERAPTOR** fossil out of stone.

Buitreraptor lived in the deserts and forests of what is now Argentina.

N
W — E
S

☐ where this dinosaur lived

BUITRERAPTOR had wings, but it could not fly. It probably couldn't jump or climb very well.

BUITRERAPTOR was about the size of a rooster.

BUITRERAPTOR had a strange head shape. Paleontologists think it helped the dinosaur catch fish and other small prey.

CAUDIPTERYX

PRONOUNCED: KAW-dip-TER-ix

NAME MEANING: tail feathers

TIME PERIOD LIVED: Early Cretaceous Period, about 125 to 122 million years ago

LENGTH: 3 feet (0.9 m)

WEIGHT: 15 pounds (7 kg)

TYPE OF EATER: omnivore

PHYSICAL FEATURES: long feathers on arms and tail, strong legs, short arms, and beak

CAUDIPTERYX swallowed rocks. The dinosaur used the rocks in its stomach to help break down food.

CAUDIPTERYX had short, feathered arms, but it could not fly. It ran and jumped.

Caudipteryx lived in the wetlands and forests of what is now China.

where this dinosaur lived

N
W E
S

CAUDIPTERYX had small, sharp teeth inside its beak. It ate plants and small animals.

DEINONYCHUS

PRONOUNCED: dye-NON-i-kus

NAME MEANING: terrible claw

TIME PERIOD LIVED: Cretaceous Period, about 118 to 110 million years ago

LENGTH: 10 feet (3 m)

WEIGHT: 110 pounds (50 kg)

TYPE OF EATER: carnivore

PHYSICAL FEATURES: traveled on two legs, as tall as an adult human

Deinonychus lived in what is now the United States.

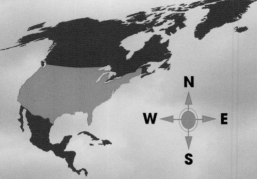

☐ **where this dinosaur lived**

N
W E
S

DEINONYCHUS probably hunted in packs.

DEINONYCHUS had a large brain and eyes. Paleontologists think the dinosaur was smart.

The Velociraptor featured in the 1993 movie *Jurassic Park* was actually modeled after DEINONYCHUS.

FALCARIUS

PRONOUNCED: FAL-car-EE-us

NAME MEANING: sickle cutter

TIME PERIOD LIVED: Early Cretaceous Period, about 125 million years ago

LENGTH: 13 feet (4 m)

WEIGHT: 220 pounds (100 kg)

TYPE OF EATER: herbivore

PHYSICAL FEATURES: long body, feathers, and long, curved claws

Falcarius lived in the prairies and forests of what is now the United States.

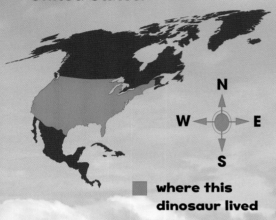

N
W E
S

■ where this dinosaur lived

FALCARIUS may have used its feathers to stay warm.

FALCARIUS' curved claws were up to 5 inches (13 centimeters) long.

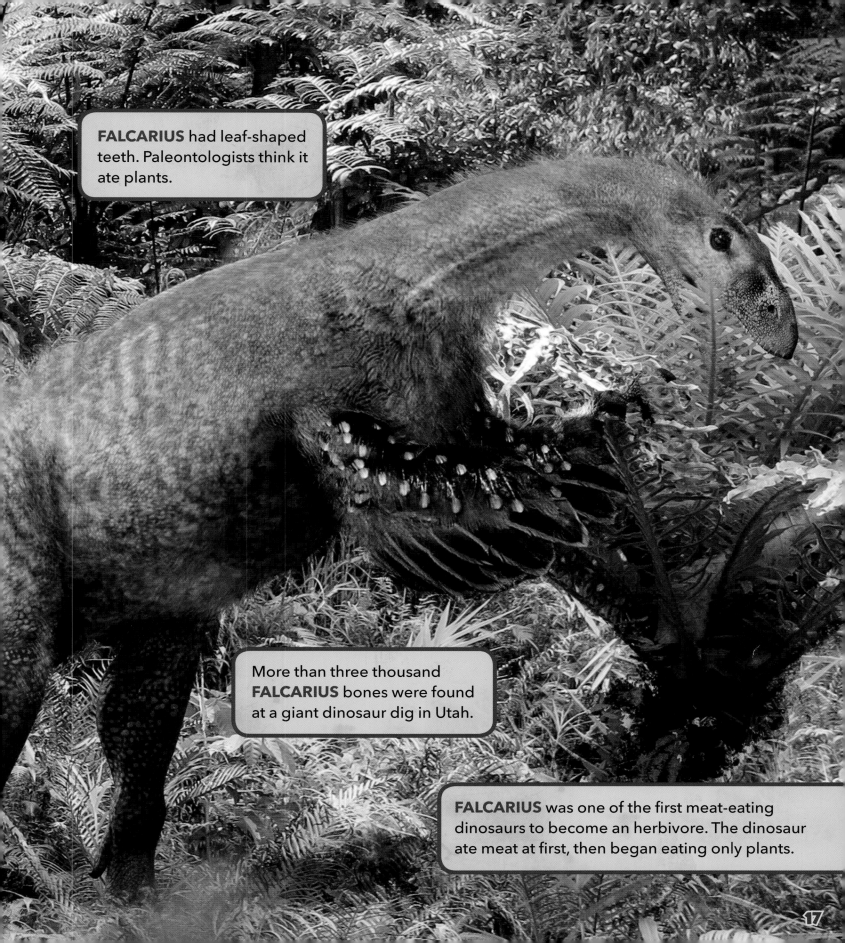

FALCARIUS had leaf-shaped teeth. Paleontologists think it ate plants.

More than three thousand **FALCARIUS** bones were found at a giant dinosaur dig in Utah.

FALCARIUS was one of the first meat-eating dinosaurs to become an herbivore. The dinosaur ate meat at first, then began eating only plants.

MICRORAPTOR

PRONOUNCED: MIKE-row-RAP-tur

NAME MEANING: tiny thief

TIME PERIOD LIVED: Early Cretaceous Period, about 125 to 122 million years ago

LENGTH: 2.5 feet (0.8 m)

WEIGHT: 1.3 pounds (0.6 kg)

TYPE OF EATER: carnivore

PHYSICAL FEATURES: traveled on two legs, covered in feathers

Like today's pelicans, **MICRORAPTOR** swallowed fish whole.

MICRORAPTOR was a small dinosaur with long feathers. Some scientists think the dinosaur looked like a giant butterfly in the distance.

MICRORAPTOR could not fly, but it may have glided from tree to tree.

Microraptor lived in the forests of what is now China.

N
W E
S

where this dinosaur lived

PROTARCHAEOPTERYX

PRONOUNCED: PROH-tar-kee-OP-ter-iks

NAME MEANING: first ancient wing

TIME PERIOD LIVED: Early Cretaceous Period, about 135 million years ago

LENGTH: 3 feet (0.9 m)

WEIGHT: 5 pounds (2 kg)

TYPE OF EATER: omnivore

PHYSICAL FEATURES: feathers, short arms, and strong legs

The dinosaur's body was about the size of a turkey.

PROTARCHAEOPTERYX could not fly. Instead it ran on its strong back legs.

At first paleontologists thought **PROTARCHAEOPTERYX** was a bird. They later discovered it was related to small feathered dinosaurs, such as Incisivosaurus.

Protarchaeopteryx lived in the wetlands and forests of what is now China.

where this
dinosaur lived

SAURORNITHOLESTES

PRONOUNCED: sore-OR-nith-oh-LESS-tease

NAME MEANING: lizard-bird thief

TIME PERIOD LIVED: Late Cretaceous Period, about 75 million years ago

LENGTH: 6 feet (1.8 m)

WEIGHT: 30 pounds (14 kg)

TYPE OF EATER: carnivore

PHYSICAL FEATURES: sharp teeth and claws, traveled on two legs

SAURORNITHOLESTES was about as long as a small dog, such as a terrier.

SAURORNITHOLESTES ate small prey, such as lizards and birds. It may have also been a scavenger.

Saurornitholestes lived in what are now the United States and Canada.

N
W · E
S

where this dinosaur lived

Like many raptors **SAURORNITHOLESTES** had a sharp claw on each back leg.

TROODON

PRONOUNCED: TROH-o-don

NAME MEANING: wounding tooth

TIME PERIOD LIVED: Late Cretaceous Period, about 74 to 65 million years ago

LENGTH: 6 feet (1.8 m)

WEIGHT: 110 pounds (50 kg)

TYPE OF EATER: carnivore

PHYSICAL FEATURES: traveled on two legs, sharp teeth and claws

TROODON had a large brain. Scientists believe it may have been one of the smartest dinosaurs.

A female **TROODON** laid two eggs at a time. She would sit on the eggs to keep them warm until they hatched.

TROODON had long, curved, and jagged teeth. They helped the dinosaur eat small animals, such as lizards and insects.

Troodon lived in what are now the United States and Canada.

N
W — E
S

where this dinosaur lived

VARIRAPTOR

PRONOUNCED: VA-ree-RAP-tor

NAME MEANING: thief from Var River

TIME PERIOD LIVED: Late Cretaceous Period, about 70 million years ago

LENGTH: 6 feet (1.8 m)

WEIGHT: 100 pounds (45 kg)

TYPE OF EATER: carnivore

PHYSICAL FEATURES: traveled on two legs, claws on hands and feet, sharp teeth

Like many raptors, **VARIRAPTOR** ran quickly on two legs.

VARIRAPTOR'S arm bones show that it could slash its prey with a lot of force.

VARIRAPTOR was a small, smart predator. It spent much of its time hunting prey.

Very few VARIRAPTOR fossils have been found.

Variraptor lived in what is now France.

where this dinosaur lived

N
W · E
S

VELOCIRAPTOR

PRONOUNCED: vuh-LOSS-eh-RAP-tur

NAME MEANING: speedy thief

TIME PERIOD LIVED: Late Cretaceous Period, about 75 million years ago

LENGTH: 6 feet (1.8 m)

WEIGHT: 33 pounds (15 kg)

TYPE OF EATER: carnivore

PHYSICAL FEATURES: feathers, sharp teeth, traveled on two legs

Velociraptor lived in central Asia, in what are now Mongolia and China.

where this dinosaur lived

VELOCIRAPTOR hunted in packs.

VELOCIRAPTOR had a curved claw on each back foot. The claw was 3 inches (7.6 cm) long.

VELOCIRAPTOR killed prey with its long, sharp claws. The dinosaur also ate dinosaur eggs. It broke the eggs open with its sharp teeth.

29

GLOSSARY

BEAK (BEEK)—the hard, pointed part of an animal's mouth

CARNIVORE (KAR-nuh-vor)—an animal that eats only meat

COMMUNICATE (kuh-MYOO-nuh-kate)—to share information, thoughts, or feelings

CRETACEOUS PERIOD (krah-TAY-shus PIHR-ee-uhd)—the third period of the Mesozoic Era; the Cretaceous Period was from 145 to 65 million years ago

FOSSIL (FOSS-uhl)—the remains of an animal or plant from millions of years ago that have turned to rock

GLIDE (GLIDE)—to move smoothly through the air; animals that glide do not flap their wings

HATCH (HACH)—to come out of an egg

HERBIVORE (HUR-buh-vor)—an animal that eats only plants

OMNIVORE (OM-nuh-vor)—an animal that eats both plants and animals

PACK (PAK)—a small group of animals that hunts together

PALEONTOLOGIST (pale-ee-uhn-TOL-uh-jist)—a scientist who studies fossils

PRAIRIE (PRAIR-ee)—a large area of flat grassland

PREDATOR (PRED-uh-tur)—an animal that hunts other animals for food

PREY (PRAY)—an animal hunted by another animal for food

PRONOUNCE (proh-NOUNSS)—to say a word in a certain way

SCAVENGER (SKAV-uhn-jer)—an animal that eats animals that are already dead

WETLAND (WET-land)—an area of land covered by water and plants; marshes, swaps, and bogs are wetlands

CRITICAL THINKING USING THE COMMON CORE

1. What was Bambiraptor named after? Use the text to help you with your answer. (Key Ideas and Details)

2. Raptors like Caudipteryx and Protarchaeopteryx were omnivores. What does "omnivore" mean? (Craft and Structure)

3. Many raptors had feathers but could not fly. Name an animal today that has feathers but can't fly. (Integration of Knowledge and Ideas)

READ MORE

Riehecky, Janet. *Velociraptor.* Little Paleontologist. North Mankato, Minn.: Capstone Press, 2015.

Silverman, Buffy. *Can You Tell a Velociraptor from a Deinonychus?* Dinosaur Look-Alikes. Minneapolis: Lerner Publications Company, 2014.

West, David. *Velociraptor and Other Raptors and Small Carnivores.* Dinosaurs! New York: Gareth Stevens Pub., 2011.

INTERNET SITES

FactHound offers a safe, fun way to find Internet sites related to this book. All of the sites on FactHound have been researched by our staff.

Here's all you do:

Visit *www.facthound.com*

Type in this code: 9781491496510

 Super-cool stuff! Check out projects, games and lots more at **www.capstonekids.com**

INDEX